Trace and write.

a a a

a a a

B B B

b b b

Attie ate apples.

Bo buys balloons.

Trace and write.

C C C

c c c

D D D

d d d

Cindy can count.

Dan dives deep.

Trace and write.

E *E*

e *e*

F *F*

f *f*

Eddie eats eggs.

Fred frog floats.

Trace and write.

G G G

g g

H H

h h

Gail gathers grapes.

Hal has a hat.

Trace and write.

$\mathcal{M}$ $\mathcal{M}$

m m

$\mathcal{N}$ $\mathcal{N}$

n n

Mia makes music.

Ned newt naps.

Trace and write.

O O

o o

P P P

p p p

Otto Owl hoots.

Pat plays piano.